THE SWEARY FLOWER MANDALA

VOL.3

Holy Shit

Adult Mandala Coloring Book for Stress Relief

COLOR TEST PAGE

COLOR TEST PAGE

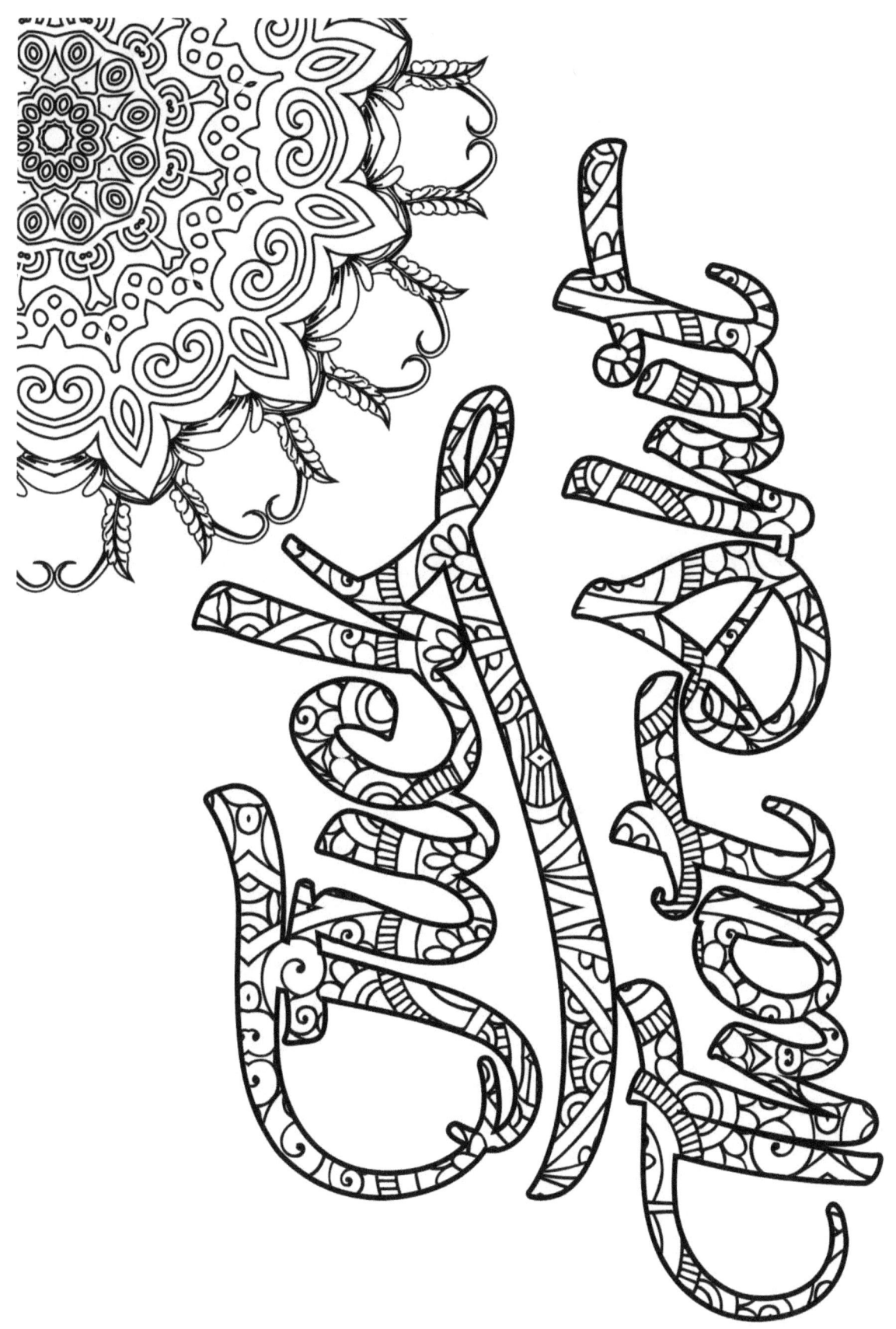

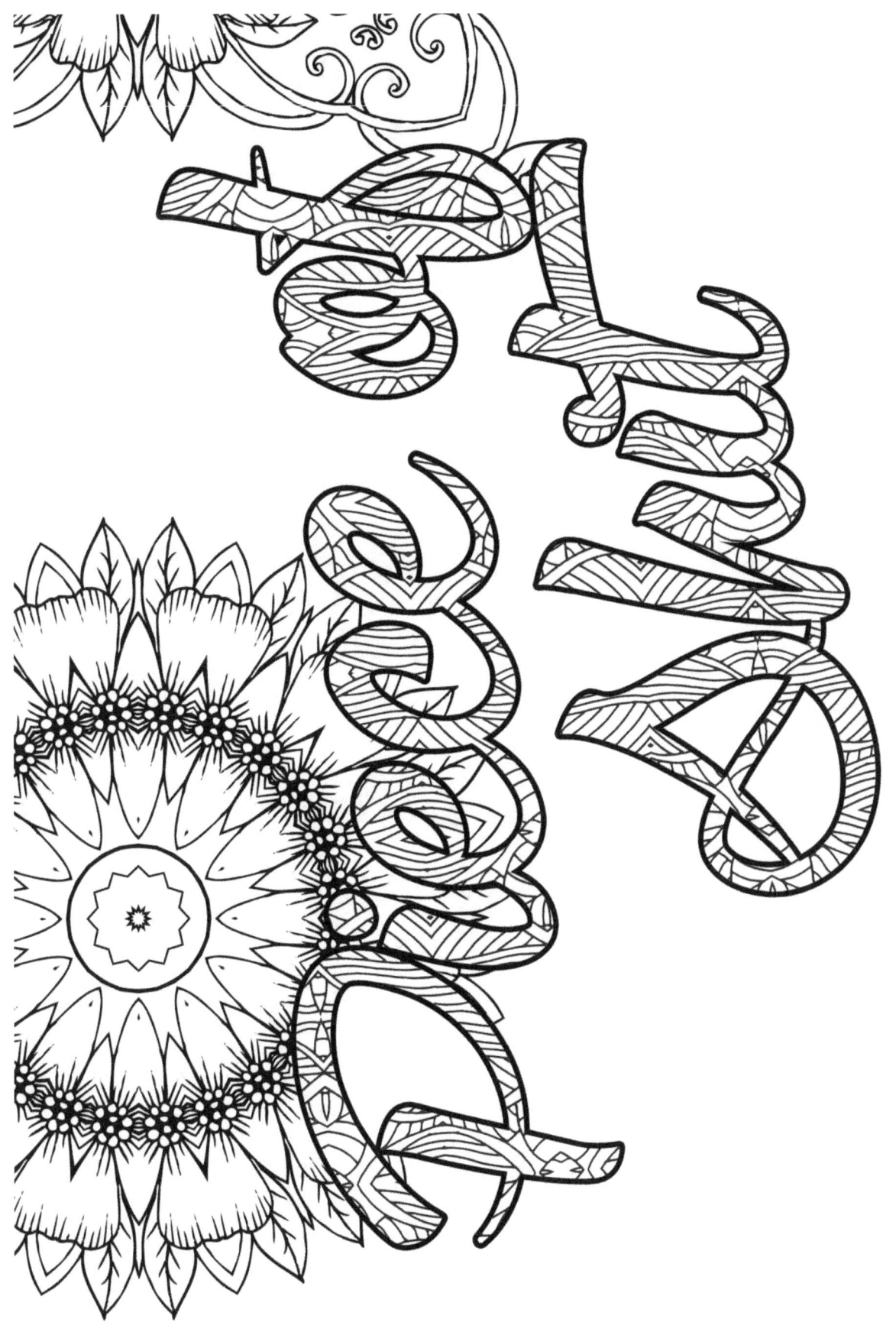

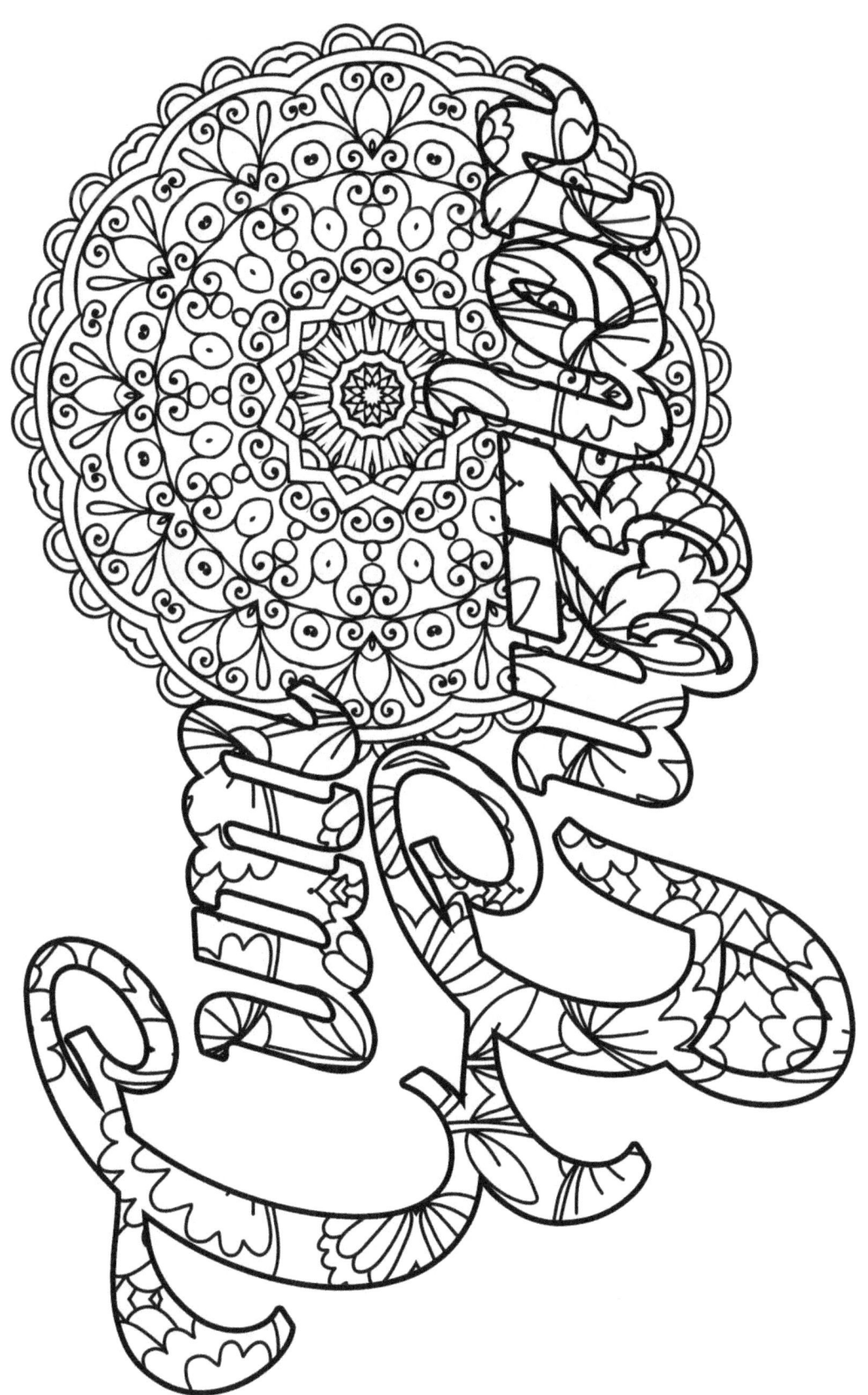

www.ingramcontent.com/pod-product-compliance
Lightning Source LLC
Chambersburg PA
CBHW080551190526
45169CB00007B/2726